Killing Ghosts

Foreword

We spend so much time running from ghosts. We wage wars against the intangible stressors that linger in our hearts and rationalize the fleeting moments of panic that we cannot explain. We fight the wrong fights and wrestle with imaginary demons.

As mothers. As women. As humans. We chase the unattainable and accept defeat when we fall short. Somewhere in our souls we know that there is a different way but we cannot see where it might take us. Maybe we aren't even sure what we're avoiding.

As I've grown into mid-life and marriage and motherhood, my perspective has shifted on almost everything. Such things tend to change people. If we're being optimistic, it's confidence. An assertiveness and sense of self that comes with age and experience. If you're as jaded as I tend to be, it's a disregard for social protocol and an overall weariness from bearing the weight of societal expectations. In short, I got tired of asking people to validate my fears and failures. I decided to stop running.

Some of it is pandemic fallout. You can't go through isolation and the utter chaos we've collectively shared—in whatever capacity—without some reflection and inner monologue. None of us are the same as we were. Not really. Even in the absence of outside forces, though, it is healthy to reevaluate. It is healthy to face the things that haunt you.

So here I am. Finding the ghosts that I've run from (maybe run to, in some cases) and killing them. Or trying to. Everything that makes a person who they are—faith, family, purpose—has been in my scope. It's hard. It's really uncomfortable to start asking questions that can turn your world upside down. To deconstruct your motivations and look at why you think and act and love the way you do. We all want to believe that what we know is real.

I believe in truth. I believe that sometimes things are black and white. There are truths that exist simply because they are true and they do not require my approval. I also believe that there are a thousand shades of gray that make the world uncertain and dynamic and confusing and beautiful.

The thing about reevaluating everything you know is that untangling untruths and misconceptions can be incredibly painful. It's hard to pull at one thread without your entire tapestry falling apart.

Here's a secret: Despite everything we've been told, it's okay to come undone. It's okay to let yourself feel the weight and stumble under it. To unravel and subsequently weave yourself into something more beautiful from time to time.

Pretending that you aren't impacted by the world around you isn't strength—it's a lie. So if everything feels heavy, you are not alone. This is all idiotically hard.

There comes a time when you have to kill your ghosts, but in order to do that you have to face them. You have to look at the ugly parts of yourself and your world. Grieve the ones that need to fall away, or celebrate their departure. Welcome the truth and the clarity.

You don't have to be haunted forever.

Dedications and Gratitude

This is for anyone who feels like they aren't enough. Or that they are too much.

For the moms who feel alone. Who feel overwhelmed. Who are worried that they are screwing everything up. For the ones who are in the trenches, just figuring out how to keep everyone alive.

For the women who are figuring out who they are again. Who are out there killing their ghosts and taking steps they are too scared to take every day.

For the Moms Who Write, who have been there for me when they didn't even know it. You are a gift.

Keep it together
But know when it's time to unravel
Nobody ever told you
That pretending it's easy isn't strength—
It's a lie we tell to make them feel better.

The Haunt

The exhaustion –
You cared. Sometimes more than you wanted to.
But not as much as you said you did.
You liked the fight, you never cried,
And you were there until you couldn't be.

Climb over withered bodies
You used to see their faces. You knew their names.
The ones you used to need,
The ones who also bought the lies
How can you care about every single thing?

The payout came too soon—
A check is cashed, a law is passed,
It's not about you—it never was.
Bleed more blood than you can give
At least you can say you tried.

- Diary of a Weary Warrior

The hourglass ran out of sand before you were ready,
And you just kept going.
Hoping that nobody would notice,
You dried up years ago.
Even though you did everything that said you should—
You thought you'd held up your end of the bargain.

You'd take it all back if you could,
But you don't know how.
It's all been going on for so long,
You ran out of faith years ago.
Why can't you put down the poison you're drinking?
You should know better by now.

Bent backwards over white sheets,
You've said the things you're supposed to say
It's too late when you realize that nothing was right.
You belong to you.
Everything you are afraid of is between you and God.
It's time to spill the poison.

- *Purity*

Her lipstick is too red,
Trying to steal the focus from tired eyes
She's learned to hide in plain sight—
At least someone needs her.

Rachel at the checkout asks how she's doing
Her lipstick twists into a smile.
"Busy as always!"
An empty laugh lets her know it's okay.

He holds the door when she leaves,
Nods a "you're welcome" without even seeing
It's been two days since he shaved
But Rachel didn't even notice.

He runs through the list
Even though he's read it a dozen times
He isn't sure how else to love her,
So he tries really hard to get this right.

Rachel smiles as he empties the cart,
And he smiles back because he knows she means it.
She asks how his day was, mostly to be polite
A million things cross his mind,
But he just says, "Busy!"

All of the things he doesn't say
Are on the tip of his tongue.
In an hour he'll go drown them in bourbon
And hope it's quiet enough to sleep tonight.

An awkward jog to the too-big car they all drive
Copied and pasted into the parking lot lines
Asphalt dotted with trees to remind them
That something out there is alive.

- *Strip Mall Serenade*

Sisyphus complex—
Trapped in the struggle
Watch the boulder roll down a thousand times
They said it would happen
So just keep trying
You'll get it one day

Strong, only for one crystalline moment
The fleeting triumph while you're on top
It feels light when everything else falls away
Someday it might occur to you
To leave the boulder at the bottom.

- Toxic Tenacity

Diamond in the rough
At least that's how I pictured myself
Nobody took the time to make me shine
No cuts, no polish
Shrouded in black, I became a lump of coal
So I put more pressure on myself
Waiting for it to become unbearable
Because if it crushes me
Someday I'll sparkle
Or that's what I believed
Pain would do.

- Diamond

You know you should care more than you do
The truth will set you on fire
But these days
You aren't sure if that's a good thing
You know you should feel more than you do
You just want to shut down
For a while
But the headlines glare at you from every screen
You know you should rest more than you do
The fatigue will make you numb
But honestly
You need a break from the rage.

- Shoulds

When you look around,
What do you find?
What lies are you hiding behind?
Is it too hard to dig deep?
Will you find your way out?
You value comfort over truth
But it always breaks down.

When you ask yourself,
What do you know?
What are the things you need to let go?
Do you ache for honesty?
Truth is hard
You don't want to know
The things that tear you apart.

Close your eyes and count to ten—
Raze the land and build again
What's real is more than what you can know
What's true is more than they're willing to show
You can find more than comfort
You can see all their lies
Ache for the honesty,
What do you see?

- *Exposition*

Everything you say stings
Tiny needles, pricking my skin
It took me years to figure out
That you were a cactus
Your spines piercing the flesh
Of anything that dared
To get too close

- *Cacti Munitions*

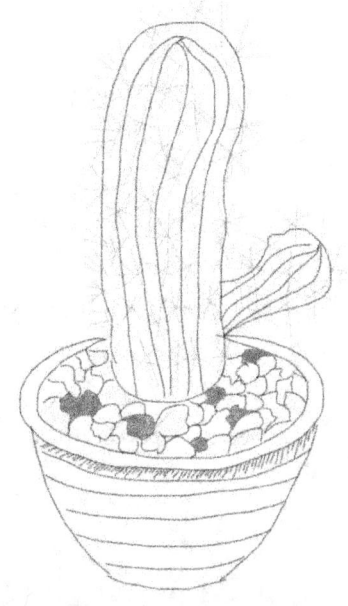

Sometimes the hardest thing
    is figuring out what you want.
You think you know,
You probably always thought you knew,
But you get it and it isn't enough.
Or it's a flat, empty version of the dream in your head
Where is the life?
You keep going, because it will be worth it—
It always is
You only get out what you put in.
That's what you heard somewhere, anyway.
What you've burned into your brain.
More hours. More work. More sacrifice.
More.
If you give everything you have,
You'll get everything you want.
But you gave everything,
And you aren't sure what it is you're supposed to get.
Is the giving enough?
What have you given to?
Will they even remember you?
You said you wanted to change the world
You got lost somewhere, though.
Your destination changed,
    but you never recharted the course.
Everything you thought you wanted got closer,
While everything you needed seemed unattainable
All you can think about is how to close the gap—
How to get there from here.
Where is the life?

Take pictures of the places you pass.
Remember where you are.
The life is there.
There is life in broken. In chaos and messes and busy.
There is life in all of it.
So rechart. and fill your sails,
Because the journey is everything you need.
The truth is this—
What you want and what you think you're supposed to
want are not the same.

- A False Destination

Curated and beautiful
You are the showpiece
Twisting and flipping and performing
Every time they turn on the lights
The job you never applied for
    but eagerly filled
They could see the all of the best parts of you
It never occurred to you they'd also want to see
What happened backstage.

- *Fish Bowl*

Tossing stones
Hoping they hit something that matters
Your righteous indignation should be enough
You can't make people care as much as they should
So you scream louder
You use stronger words
Igniting flames
To set the world on fire.

When everything ignites
You realize you live there too
Watching it burn hurts—
Sure, they deserved it
They didn't care as much as they should
Haze and questions linger
Shrouding everything that's left.

You can't weave a world from rage
You can't rebuild with what's left
So you're tossing stones again
Hoping that they'll hit something that matters.

- Thrown

Your anxious minds are a drug for me. I thrive on it. I prey on it. Every pang of humanity that emanates from your fragile bodies is a hit - tears and fear course through my veins like heroin.

When I saw you there, the smell of your insecurity was intoxicating. It wafted easily through the pallid, delicate veil of confidence that you spent your whole life crafting. The useless shroud was barely enough to keep you alive. You struggled to believe what you saw when I descended, and your hesitation was a gift. It's always easier when you're not expecting me.

Your mind was an embarrassing swirl of humiliation and defeat, ravenously consuming any glimmer of light that dared to enter. The darkness is my favorite place to dwell; it was so easy to hide in your shadows. Your own mind created this putrid place—this greenhouse for all things ghastly.

One by one, I stripped the glimmer from your internal world, the illumination dimming until there was nothing left to see. It didn't take long for the light to die completely. By the time you realized I was there, it was much too late.

It's time to take your shimmer somewhere else.

- Letter From My Anxiety

She can't win when there's no finish line
A glass ceiling broken by design
She didn't know why
She was supposed to want those things
Nobody ever bothered to tell her.

- Sins of Omission

Peel it away -
> Layer by layer

So raw you start to bleed
What's it like to have what you need?

Rip it to shreds -
> Page by page

Put the story back together
Words that bind, songs that tether

What if you can -
> What if you are

Whatever you believed
Maybe that's what you're supposed to grieve.

- Whatever You Believed

Life doesn't happen easily anymore
They tell me again that it's worth it.
I'll never miss what I don't know
It isn't mine to find, anyway

You have it all and still can't grow,
    Because you don't know what else to be
Inside the walls you hide the unraveling,
Drowning in Facebook and wine

You're grateful but empty
Hungry when you have plenty
Inside the walls you hide the unraveling
What's out there for you to find?

- *Thirst*

How are you doing?
I'm okay.
I have everything I need.
We're hanging in there.
How are you holding up?
I'm tired of telling lies
But I still say
I'm okay.
Better than we could be.
I don't say
That I would give up okay
If it meant that I didn't have to feel alone.
So I'm okay. Today.
But not okay enough
To pretend I don't need to breathe the same air as you

- Grateful

I wanted to listen
But nothing made sense.

The words tumbled into the air
Clumsy and hurtful
You could have meant well—
You probably didn't.

I wanted to listen
But nothing was said.

Your voice was louder than everyone else
Sharp and relentless
You didn't say anything
But you said it with conviction.

I wanted to listen
But there was nothing to hear.

- *An Attempt Was Made*

Mouths that crush
Tongues lashing, destroying
Forgive them for they know not what they do
I pretend that's true
It's the only thing that lets me keep my faith.
- *Among Monsters*

My eyes can't take
All the light you cast aside
You still flicker like a flame
In the darkness you shine
The shadows you cast are where I hide

So I turn out the light

If seeing is believing
Then I don't believe in anything
That's okay for a while
For now I need my lie

So I turn out the light

- *Flipped*

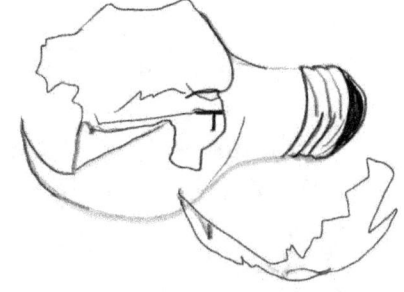

We declare wars
Against things we can't see
The outrage that loiters in our chests
We rationalize fleeting moments that we cannot explain

We fight the wrong battles
And wrestle with imaginary demons.

Mothers, women, humans—
We all chase the unattainable
Then surrender when we fail
We pick up more than we can carry
And wonder why we drop the load

We declare the wrong enemies
And wrestle with imaginary demons.

Step after step toward an end
We don't know what we don't know
We can't see where the victory could take us
Somewhere in our souls we know there is a different way

We declare the wrong enemies
And wrestle with imaginary demons.

- *Demons We Can't See*

The words
I remember every one
Someone told me not to let them under my skin
I'm not sure I know what that means
They carved their insecurities
Into me with sharpened tongues
Stealing every ounce of worth
They could find in my presence
The voices
That's what I remember
I was too afraid to look at their eyes
The words etched into my memory
Because we only remember the things that hurt
Maybe it's survival—
A way to avoid the words that scarred

- *Vampires Drain More Than Blood*

The Exorcism

Illumination
A delicate situation
The path of those who are seen
When you scorch the earth you can't go back
Memories you bury and burn

Now brighter than before—
A naiveté that saves
The glow of the unsure,
Where your questions mean more
Than any answer you can find

The spark in the dark
A flash so faint you question it
It's enough, though
Because the light means more
Than anything you find in the black

The shadow was safe
Until it swallowed you whole
The darkness of the unknown
But your questions still mean more
Than any answer you can find.

- Illume

Life breaks your heart.

Things are harder than they should be because people are messy and this is all complicated. We walk around, doing the best that we can, making the decisions we know how to make and hoping that it's all enough. We crash into each other and there is conflict or synergy and it's impossible to know which you'll find until you've already collided.

Sometimes everything is fine, and then it isn't. Maybe it was something in your control; a mistake that you made or a decision you made that resulted in something unexpectedly painful. Or maybe it was something entirely beyond your control.

At the end of the day—how much does it matter? When your heart is broken, you want to search for whys. It is in our nature to want to figure out what happened so we can place blame appropriately. Nothing can be fixed until you figure out why it's broken in the first place, and you want to be fixed. The problem, though, is that sometimes things are just painful. Sometimes there's nobody to blame. The diagnosis. The job loss. A pandemic that derails all of your plans. A death that came too soon. A relationship that is fraying around the edges, no matter how hard you try to weave everything back together.

Right now, my heart is broken. And while I wait for it to heal, it is tempting to lash out. I want to be angry or frustrated. To self-medicate and self-indulge, because I am hurting and I want it to stop right now. Self-care is important, but so much of what we call self-care is not self-care at all.

It is not bubble baths and wine and trash television. It isn't junk food or isolation. Sometimes, those things can help, for a minute. None of them heal.

So, when my heart is broken, I try to wait. I have to feel the pain first; I have to locate it in order to treat it. Wrapping it up in bandages without caring for it first is going to lead to festering and death. You cannot simply cover a wound and wait for it to go away.

It was only recently that I understood what people meant when they said they felt "gutted." That consuming physical manifestation of emotional hurt that starts in the abdomen and shoots violently up into your chest, tearing through you with surprising speed. I wasn't sure if I wanted to scream or cry or throw up, and I found myself wondering if it's even possible to do all of those things at the same time. There is nothing pretty about this.

But I felt it. And now I know where my hurt is. I can name it and look it in the face. Maybe this is a fight I'll lose. And that's okay. I'm more than this moment. My story is bigger than this chapter. And nobody stays broken forever if they don't want to. Get uncomfortable. Clean the wounds and let them mend. Get uncomfortable.

Life breaks your heart. But it will also heal it.

- *When Your Heart Is Broken*

A dread I feel in my bones
Nothing ever goes like I think it will go
But I show up again
Pieces of me rattle and crack
Every break feels like the last.

The pieces are so small they start to get lost
And never quite fit back together
Unimportant, insignificant
The things I forget I need
Slivers of salvation
Buried in the debris.

The frenzy you thrived on is unsustained
A relic of your manic survival
Some day the dust will settle
If I let it all die here
This break could be the last.

- Slivers of Salvation

Roots and vines
Existence that binds
You grow where you shouldn't
Easy and consistent

The rain flooded you,
But you never went under
Holding fast
Tethered to the dirt in the storm

The sun ravaged you
But you never burned
Your leaves were green
As the world wilted and withered

The shade starved you
But you never faded
Greener than everything else
Even when it all went dark

Roots and vines
Existence that binds
You grow where you shouldn't
Resilient and wild

- *Ivy*

The space between
Birth and death
Dust and breath and stars
Where moons collided
Atmospheric scars
You screamed for so long
You used up all your air
By the time you could speak again
No one was there
You learned to burn and never die
And somehow fall but never fly
In the cold emptiness,
You're the flame and the wild
A path through the space between
Beginning and end
Dust and breath and stars
Where worlds collided
The universe is ours.

- *Nebula*

I didn't know I was lost
I spent time alone
I knew my own voice
At least I thought I did
I just didn't know I had anything to say
Sometimes I read too much
Or drank too much
Or drowned myself in him
But I knew what I was doing
Or I thought I did
Sometimes I do what I know isn't right
Sometimes I'd rather lie than fight
That night you tried to find me
I couldn't find myself.

- *Discover Me*

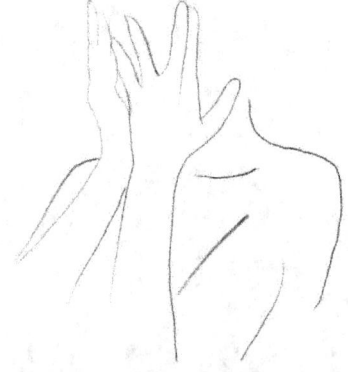

Sometimes to say goodbye isn't entirely sad.

The time I left the place that kept me too busy to breathe.
The time I wanted to say no and I actually said it. I was
alone after that but it was not a sad goodbye.
The time I shut the door and it was quiet enough to hear
myself think for the first time in days.
The time I said goodbye to the me that was too tired and
too angry and too scared. I don't miss her either.
The time I left before the storm was able to drown me. The
black skies raged in my rear view. That was a perfect
goodbye.

Sometimes to say goodbye isn't entirely sad.

- Farewell Face

It was hot—so hot my dress stuck to my thighs as my heels clicked on the cracked concrete.

I'm not sure what was different. Maybe it was the moon or the music or the crowd.

Or it could have been the whiskey.

Either way, I opened the door to an empty house and decided I was done.

The picture I painted for everybody else. The songs I wrote and the stories I told to make me more.

But why would I lie when I hate how it feels?

Why do I give to a world that steals?

When I pulled my lashes off my face and ripped the extensions out of my hair I felt naked.

It's strange to feel like I don't exist when I put the illusion away.

It was so cold—so cold that I could feel my blood slow down in my veins.

A march toward new, from black to blue

The emptiness becomes an open wound

The life I lived for everyone else somehow made me even more alone.

How can I soar when I forgot how to crawl?

Why would I give my best to a ghost?

When I put the clothes away and washed the makeup off my skin I felt naked.

I want to feel like I exist when I put the illusion away.

So in my bed, I declare a silent war.

Killing the ghosts I've brought along for the ride.

- *Killing Ghosts*

The paint faded,
      Peeling and worn
Rough wood trimming tired walls
Shades of blue and gray
Flowers add color to the illusion
Pretending that if you try hard it won't seem so dead

Empty stores and broken windows
Cinder blocks where steps should be
You forget how many years you've been away
Everything looks older, but the same

The roads are dusty
      Cracked and pitted
Fruit stands lining winding streets
The wind is steady
Gray skies and rainy nights
Somehow, even when you leave,
You don't escape the haze

Empty promises and broken dreams
All you wanted was to leave
Nostalgia brings you back again
And some sort of obligation
You've outgrown this place
But part of you will never leave.

- *Hometown*

Tiny fires
Just enough to light the way
Carefully staked on the sidelines
Flickers that cast wobbly shadows
And show you everything you need to know
Just barely

Casting shadows on fuzzy paths
No one told you which way to go
And you can't see what's next,
You have no idea how it ends
Nothing but flickers and wobbly shadows
That only show you what you need to know

But you can see the next step
Most of the time, anyway
Even though you still trip on the stones
And you're thankful for the lamp lighters
Tiny fires
Just enough to light the way.

- *Lamplighter*

The jungle that sprung up around you
Is suddenly more than you can manage
This thing you created is too big
      Too loud
          Too much
It's a wild you can't contain
You don't really want to
You aren't supposed to box it in
Any more than you're supposed to tear it down
The jungle that closed in around you
A tangle of all the things that you love
      The things that you fear
          The things that you are
It's a wild you can't ever contain.

- *The Wild*

For once you'd like to open your eyes
Without being yanked into consciousness
You wake up and somehow you're already late
Every day, you try to find another way
Another way to fit it all in.

Everything takes so much longer than it should.
You never stop moving, but at the end of the day you aren't
any closer to being done.
Your energy doesn't last as long as your day.
It's easy to tell yourself to take a break,
But every time you do you get so overwhelmed by what is
waiting when you get back—
The work doesn't stop because you do.

So you just keep moving, looking for any help you can find.
Looking for something easier.
You know it shouldn't be this way.
And people try to offer advice
As if you haven't already spent hours. Days. YEARS trying
to do things differently.

It seems so much easier for everybody else.
If you could just get up earlier
If you could just focus
If you could just be faster.
Or smarter.
Or less overwhelmed.
If you could just be more,
It would all get done.

But it never ends.

Not because you aren't enough, but because there will always be more to do.

So stop. Go slow, if you need to
And know that you aren't alone.
You aren't the only one that feels like minutes, hours, days just evaporate
And leave nothing to show for the exhaustion.
Let go.
Let go of your made up obligations and your self-imposed deadlines.
You'll get there when you get there.
And you deserve to enjoy the journey.

- Timelapse

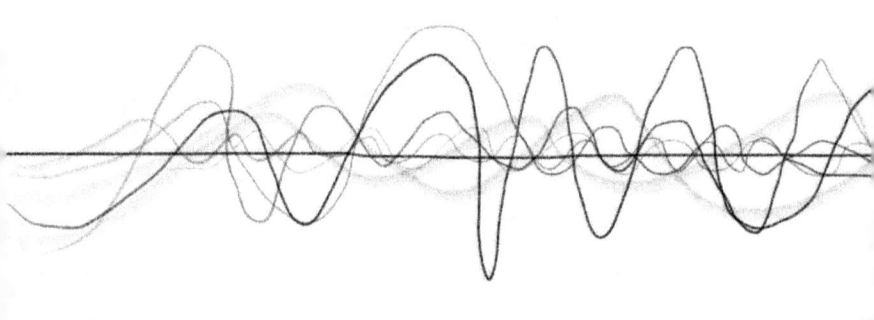

A vibration that rings in between
Not quite where I want it to be
My whole body feels the dissonance
The song that plays just barely out of tune
A melody that falls flat
I waited for the note to ring true
A sour note they tried to call blue
It wasn't meant to sound like this
My body absorbs the dissonance
Bending the melody
From blue to true
At some point I realized
The encore shouldn't take this long.

- Discord

Nothing is ever enough.

Not for me. Not for the world.

The hours I spend preparing and caring and surviving.

The work.

There is always more work than I know how to do.

When I stop, the guilt and shame I feel sit on my chest—

They choke the accomplishment out of my days.

Even when I try to will them away they linger.

Cast shadows on the brighter moments

    The ones I want to savor.

In my soul I know that rest is okay.

That without a chance to restore and replenish

    my soul will die.

Wilt and wither away in starvation.

Every dream ever been born inside my chest will expire,

Never nurtured.

Somewhere along the way I began to glorify burnout.

Why do I justify taking time for things that heal?

I know it's a broken world that praises self destruction,

    But I cling to the societal badge of honor.

The escape of "not having enough time."

Because if everyone knows how busy I am,

    maybe they'll forgive me.

Maybe they won't be so upset when I drop a ball I
desperately tried to catch.

Sometimes I wonder if I know what it's like to rest.

How would it feel to close my eyes and just go to sleep?

No cacophony in my brain.

No anxiety-induced wake ups,

    Forcing me to resolve problems that don't exist.

Rest.

I know there will be even more to do if I stop moving

So I keep going—

My body becoming a poorly maintained perpetual motion
 vehicle that crumbles under the weight.

Basking in the praise as I feel myself break.

They ask how I do it all and I want to scream that I don't.

It isn't ever finished and I don't think it ever will be,

And that fear of failure is all that keeps me going
sometimes.

Because I desperately want to be enough.

In my soul, though, I know that I'm okay.

That without a chance to restore and replenish and feed my
soul will die.

So I add myself to the list

And hope that the rest of it feels less daunting.

- Add Me To The List

Edge dancing -
Kicking rocks to see how far they fall
Something about the drop makes you feel small
I'm afraid I'll hit the bottom -
But what if I fly?
Is it better to stay alive
But never leave the precipice?
I wait for someone to push me
Wondering ifI'll soar.
Fear and uncertainty—
They're kind of the same
Does it hurt any less ifI give it a name?
Every piece I kick into the abyss
Is a piece I give away
A bit of myself
Every piece I lose to my pain
Is a piece that can heal
If I fly.

- *Edge Dance*

Someone told us we can do it all. Reality falls somewhat short of that, though. We talk about balance as if we know what that feels like. For me it feels like juggling while someone just keeps tossing more balls into your hands.

And I don't know how to juggle.

For a while, we're okay. At some point, things start to collide and crash around us. We have to decide which of the balls can be dropped.

Someone told us we can do it all. So we try and then we fail.

We feel defeated when we cannot keep it all together. We think we're missing something that everyone else has.

But here's the secret: Nobody has all of the balls in the air. We make choices and some things grow and others die. As we grow in and out of different stages of our lives, our priorities change alongside our whys.

Someone told us we can do it all. But what if we choose to do a few things well?

What if we thrive instead of survive? Balance is just a series of tradeoffs. Knowing which balls to juggle or drop.

- *Equilibrium*

You're so tired.
The kind of tired that sleep doesn't fix.
The tired you feel all the way through your bones.
You thought you'd be a lot further along by the time you
turned 30. 35. 40.
Things look nothing like you thought they would look.

You want to be a whole person again.
But in between snacks and laundry and hearing your name
four thousand times a day
You can't seem to find all of the pieces.

Every time you let a dream die
Another piece disappears
And there is a dusty vacuum where dreams used to be.

But you're still so tired.
The kind of tired that sleep can't fix.

The ache that twists its way into every waking moment
And you start to wonder
—if this is how it's always going to be...

If the person you were is now a snack fixing, taxi driving,
anxiety ridden, sleep deprived shell
Who is always looking for the rest of her pieces.

And they tell you not to blink, but there are days
when you can barely hold your eyes open.

You thought you'd be better at this.

But right now, here, use these seconds to take a break
Breathe. Cry if you need to.
And let me remind you that you are whole.

Already.

In the midst your chaotic, disorganized, yelling, living for
nap time day.

You are everything you need to be.

Even when you're tired.

- *Finding Your Pieces*

I try not to feel it
When I think someone else will know
The sinking in my gut
That comes when I'm alone
The ache of pretending
I try not to feel it

Isolation is a prison
Shame lingers in my desperation
Should it feel like this to be alone?
I know there's beauty in my broken
Strength in my devotion
Wisdom in the words I've spoken

Freedom lies in those charcoal places
The ones hidden from all of their faces
The secret room where I can be too much
Too big, too small, too crushed
The ache of loneliness
Is the absence of their rejection
I try not to feel it

- *Liberation Through Loneliness*

Legions of drummers and thieves
Rhythm and pleas
A thumping inside that makes you believe
A pounding that reverberates up your spine
Propelling you forward when you want to be still
You move even though you don't know how
You believe even when it feels impossible
A thumping inside that makes you hold on
Legions of liars and beggars and ghosts
Their marches trampling the guideposts
A liturgy you recite in your sleep
Safety in the words and the beat

- Rhythm and Revival

Sometimes,
I cannot see through the open door
There is always something in the way.
When I stretch I can see glimpses—
A hallway.
A window.
Ghosts I've been trying to run away from
For longer than I can remember.
The door was locked,
Mostly because I wanted to hide behind it.

When it opened
I felt stuck in this room
Surrounded by the things
That I thought were safe.
Ambition. Rules.
The routine that slowly destroys.
False security that I wore like a blanket
I drank it like wine
Lulling myself to sleep
Through hazy half-truths

Sometimes
I cannot see through the door
Because there is always something in the way
But the steps are easier every time
Inching my way through the shoulds
The coulds
The woulds
Toward the ghosts I was so scared of
A locked door was a lie I hid behind

Nothing is safe
But that is the thrill.
The magic.
The enchantment of purpose
Of love.
When that door opened I looked at the room
The dingy walls—
The safety that kept me at bay.

Sometimes
Slaying ghosts is safer
Than the security blanket we suffocate in.

- *The Thrill of Execution*

Keep it together,
Hold on until your fingers fail
Nobody ever told you
That it's okay to come undone
Every once in a while.

The weight you carry is real
It's okay to let yourself stumble under it
When your knees buckle
And you hit the ground
It's time to pray or rest
To unravel every thread
All of the wonder and color and magic
The dull and the frayed and the weak
Weave them into a new tapestry.

Keep it together
But know when it's time to unravel
Nobody ever told you
That pretending it's easy isn't strength—
It's a lie we tell to make them feel better.

- *Tapestry*

Roots and wings and pretty things
I'm the bird
Ride the wind—it's easier not to know where
So I never ask
Aimless, reckless, bare
Your rules don't matter—not for me
But that's my fear you see.

Only the birds are free
Or we used to be
I lost my wings somewhere down here,
Taking up a little less air

Branches grow until they break
There's only so much they can take
It's the closest we come to the sky
Only the birds are free

The weight of the roots is too much now
Anchor too long and you drown
Your rules don't matter—not for me
But that's my fear you see.

The air in my wings and other pretty things
I'm the bird
Ride the wind—it's easier not to know where
Above the branches, broken and bare
Taking up all of the air

- *Only The Birds Are Free*

I waited for the boy who fell from the stars
Because I thought
He was the only one that could be enough
Shrouded in the light I was trying to find

When I found him
I learned that he was just a broken as me

Burned by the stars
Lonely and cold
Unlearning everything
He'd been told by the universe

When I learned him
I saw that he was just as broken as me

- Starfall

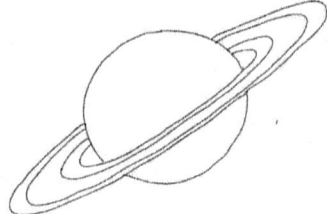

It's so easy to get lost in your hard.

The irony of yelling when all I want is a moment of peace is not lost on me.
Some days, I wish I could take back the things that tumble out of my mouth. The anger or frustration or exhaustion.

I spend so many hours wishing I had more time alone, but every moment I'm alone I'm thinking about you.

Steely eyes with a ring of gold, you see the world the way I wish I could. The way I would if I didn't drown myself in busy and tired.

The best days are the days that I breathe—sit with you and try to be. To see the things that you see around you.
And the best nights are the nights I can barely stay awake after you drift off.

Today, we laughed more than we cried. And I sat with you until you fell asleep to ocean sounds, curled beneath your favorite lights with a book you've read a thousand times.

Nothing about this part is hard.

I try to live here, even if it's only sometimes.
Because the world of trucks and planets and mystery will soon become so much more like the one I know.

And it's so easy to get lost in my hard.

- *The Hard*

You are still free in a way that I won't ever remember. You know you are fierce.

Bright and unapologetic in your need.

You created a finish line only you can see—you'll cross it a hundred times before I know it's there.

These days of survival. Chasing. Running in circles every time you decide to change direction. They are unending and draining and I know I'll never keep up, because you'll go further than I ever get to go.

I say my job is to keep you alive, but I've never seen a creature more full of life. I only need to protect it.

The stars that burst from your smile are white hot and endless. Bright and unapologetic.

When I met you I learned that I just had to hold on, and now the only thing I know is that I don't ever want to tame you.

- Relentlessly Alive

It's so easy to stray off-course.
And some days, I wish I could find my way back to where
you are right now—
The joy and love and possibility

I spent so many years trying to get where I am,
But where you are is so much better.

- I Took A Turn Somewhere

What's the world
　　But a kaleidoscope quest?
A repositioning of the things you knew
Changing and twisting and transforming
Every time you hold it up to the light.

Revolution and evolution—
It's never the same thing twice
Haphazard magnificence that is always changing
Kaleidoscope worlds colliding.

- *Kaleidoscope Quest*

Thank you to my husband, and children. You are the reason I can do anything and you bring me more joy than I knew existed.

I love you with everything I am and everything I am trying to be.

Allie Gravitt is based in Marietta, Georgia. She lives in a house full of little humans and animals and green things that she tries really hard to keep alive.

Mostly just really loves being surrounded by life in the form of people, creatures, vegetation, or art.

This is her second published poetry collection.